WINTERS
NEVER
LAST

WINTERS NEVER LAST

David Tensen
and Friends

POETRY CHAPEL
PRESS

Author website: www.davidtensen.com
Author email: david@davidtensen.com

Poetry Chapel Press
Brisbane, QLD, Australia

Cover Illustration: Copyright © 2022 David Tensen

Edited: Felicia Murrell & Rachel Huckel

Also available in eBook.

Winters Never Last / David Tensen. -- 1st ed.
ISBN 978-0-6489893-6-3

Dedicated to those

who are learning

that each season

makes way

for the next,

even the grieving winter.

Table of Contents

Poetry Chapel Collective
Contributing Authors

Deborah Blythe

Lisa Dodge Pinkham

Amanda Dzimianski

Vivien Firth

Suzy George

Kate Hughes

Kate Kim

Keally Kweyama

Marianne Lienard

Elizabeth Ma

Kate Rife

Katy Roth

Joyce Soe

Catherine Sharpe-Lewis

INTRODUCTION

Life has a way of exposing our longings for more than it has to offer across a lifetime. It is no wonder, for millennia, man has obsessed with themes of life beyond this corporeal life. After all, who would willingly choose to enter a creation of inescapable seasons of life, loss, and liminality? We experience springs and summers ripe with budding life, but also autumns and winters rife with fallow loss.

Thankfully, life is not a constant suffering existence. Most people are born with an innate capacity to find and create beauty in the midst of things. Along with poets past and present, I feel it is our primary task to offer the world both language and solidarity through our work. For this reason, I no longer see poetry as a luxury, but a vital necessity in naming, healing, and celebrating all of life's complexities.

After the success of Poetry Chapel™ Volume 1: The Saving I Need, I felt it was only right to invite another fourteen emerging poets to write a second Poetry Chapel™ collection with me. Again, poetry brought a diverse company of people from around the globe together to explore and express their experiences, and hold them out to the hands and hearts of strangers.

This book is made up of two halves. The first half is a collection of my own poems. If you have followed my work for a while, I suspect you'll see a progression of speech and perspectives as my own life unfolds. I continue to learn, grow, and change as I age, raise young adults, and explore the intersection between wisdom, love and faith.

As much as I hope my poems resonate with you, I lay them before you as an offering. Take. Eat. Or, pass them by.

The second half are poems the Poetry Chapel™ poets wrote and chose. Some were written during our time together and others pre-date the collective's partnership. Each poet was asked to provide a short bio and allotted six pages for poetry. If you read carefully, you will notice that a good number of the co-authors had recently lost someone close to them. Hence, their is a wide and wise spectrum of grieving in their work. For this reason, I truly believe this collection will land as a lifebuoy in the hands of many who need a voice of hope and reprieve in their own losses.

Much love,

David Tensen
www.davidtensen.com

If any poems or sections of this book were an
encouragement or help to you, I'd love to hear from you.
Email me at david@davidtensen.com.

Small Poems on God

Sinister

I'm not trying to put words in God's mouth.

My intentions are far more sinister.

I want to climb inside
with pen and paper
and write poems on why
the words fall out.

Holy Spirit

When she finds me napping
or numb to what matters,
she carefully positions
her face
a breath away
from mine.
And when I wake
(or if she prods)
the first thing I see
is her come-and-play smile.

Dust

I'd like to say
I'm always attuned
and lockstep with my Rabbi -

But we both know
that's untrue.

And yet,
His love and holding,
not scorn and scolding,
keep me chasing dust
and foraging for footprints.

Forever

This is perhaps
the most offensive
and beautiful
of all conspiracies,
   that whether or not
   I give my life
   in service to You
   and the world You love,
Your mercy endures forever.

How to Bend

Oh God,
Broken as you were
For the least of me
By the beast of me
Teach me, please
How to bend
Without breaking
Beyond repair
In this
Beautifully
Brittle
Broken
World

Shadow

Religious rules
cast a shadow
only worth following
on the path
to the warm shadow
cast by God.

And you will know
you have found
Love's wings
by the freedom you feel
to fall
without
breaking.

This Day

This day
I remember that day
you hung. Skin strung,
head heavy, breathing unsteady
holding in yourself
everything in us that is dying,
lost and grieving -
telling us we are not alone
and you are not removed
from our suffering.
Telling us
salvation stretches
beyond separation
and stands in solidarity
with the rugged beauty
of our humanity.

Fist

About your gentle hand that holds me,
do you mind making a fist
and pushing your knuckle
deep into this knot
where the fascia gathered years ago
and is holding all these memories?

God and Prayer

This Line

Despite the decades,
I still struggle to discern
       between
the steering voice
 of God
and the stirring voice
 of others
with their good intent,
persuasive prose,
and fear-laden facts.

God knows
I don't pray daily;
my Bible hardly budges
and I gave tithing away
some time ago.

In many ways,
I have become the person
I once frowned upon and feared:
A rule breaker. Bankrupt and
broken but still bold enough
to call themselves a 'believer'

or
a bond servant, of sorts,
held to God's breast
by grace and love
which I've tested
to be eternal
and true.

Yes, I am that free man
who once drew the line,
walked the line,
but now questions any line
that doesn't fall
in places of pleasure,
regardless
of who scribes it
with their speech.

Prince of Peace

Prince of Peace, please
Place your assuring hands
Upon my shoulders
And peer through
My windowed eyes
Into my worthy soul.

Prince of Peace, please
Locate the troubled places
I have no words for,
Cannot reach
Or mend on my own.

Prince of Peace, please
Pay attention to these parts.
Sometimes, things break inside
Because of unwelcome guests.
But you are very welcome
To work miracles
And heal whatever you desire.

I Am Not God

some things will come to you
in the womb
at no expense:

heartbeat
hair colour
hip size

then,
there are things
you find yourself
in:

families
fortunes
feuds

it is beyond me
how much grace
I've wasted
working to change
things beyond me:

opinions
others
origins

so much could be saved
if I could only,
for a long moment,
remember: I am not God.

If You Must, Deconstruct

If you must,
deconstruct.

Take every part:
weigh, measure,
keep and discard
necessary things.

Take all the time
you need. But
do not camp
in the ruins.

Discuss discoveries
but
do not raise monuments
to your brilliance -
brave as you may be.

Instead,
in time,
build something new.

Take the remains,
sorrows and pains,
new friends you've gained
and build something new,

allowing
the wise few
to remind you
there is a time
to break down
and a time
to build up.

The Incarnation

Take all your hope and longing,
cover it in blood, urine, faeces, straw.
Cut the cord to your dreams
with a field knife or clenched jaw.

Here lay the King of the Jews.
Crowned between thighs,
Held in arms of exhaustion.
Bathed with tears, sweat
and the soft tones
of a mother
singing songs
of deliverance
between breaths
as the King of Glory
feeds folded at her breast.

What newborn would you not
bend a knee for? What labouring mother
would not make room for life? Here's how God
chose to be with His beloved;
in a state of utter surrender
and dependence.

making His way into the world
through a uterus. Trading a heavenly crown
for one of mucus. Later, finding
woven thorns pushed in its wet place as,
once again, God surrenders
to the fulness of humanity's mess -
reconciling it all
to Himself,
counting no soul's sin
against them.

Poetic Prayer for the Weary

I am tired
And in this flurried moment
I am reminded
That you, Jesus,
You know
This life
Can be relentless.
And reaching intentional rest
Can be a tough
And lonely climb.

I know the scriptures
Promise me both
Strength and rest
When I need them -
And I acknowledge
The gift of both.
But I also acknowledge
We are all
Wonderfully different,
And that other people's rhythm
Won't always suit my song.

So, I think
What I need most
Is the wisdom you offer
To seek and to spend
Both strength and rest
In the right portions
At the right times
Without guilt or pride.
Without comparison
Or needing to justify
The way I am created
And loved by You.

Poetic Prayer for the Grieving

It comforts me
And troubles me to know
That you are acquainted with it,
Grief, that is.

Why the God of the Universe
Chose to know
And remain so close
To a time-stopping
Heart-dropping
Smile-swapping
Emotion
Is beyond me.

But I'm glad you are,
So close, that is.

Grief reminds me
Of my frailty and
The temporary nature
Of all things.
And how in those moments
Of wailing and tears
I add myself
To the eternal choir of creatures
Mourning their losses
And the measurable mortality
of this life.

Sons and Days

To My Son: On Dating and I Dos

A woman's body is not yours, son.
And yours not hers.
Never forget,
  she's not yours to possess.

Before you hold her
  to your hip,
hold her in your heart, son
  in love.
  in adoration.
  in mutual respect.

A woman is not a goal to score
  or wild sea to tame.
Never claim her
  as a notch on your belt
  or someone you nailed;
  this would only tell me
  your masculinity
  has divorced
  your humanity.

Hollywood holds no light
  to the ragged beauty
  of true togetherness.

Love and lust and sex
  are terribly messy, son.
They are fragile
  and break often;
  this is normal.
Invest in your soul, son.
Do not throw it
  to the wind,
  or any woman
  who throws herself
  at your feet.

Wait. Wait for those
  worthy of your fine heart.

You'll learn lots as you go
  through joy, pain and elation.
Just promise me, son
  you'll go slow
  making every date
  and 'I Do' count
  for both of you.

Father's Day

On a day like this
when you celebrate
and lavish me
with socks, chocolate and cards made in class
it's easy to assume
that I deserve the applause
for all I am and have done
- and perhaps it's true,
after all
you carry
the same DNA
and dare I say
every tendency I have
to overestimate
my ability to know
what is best for you.

But you should know
you have been
without a doubt
the ones who shaped me
with your very being.
And God knows
it has been a gift
to raise you,
and still is.

You caused me
to grow up
in more ways than I have words for;
but can I just say
in reply to your thank yous,
Thank you.

Australia Day

I'd like for this day
to be more than it is
but the more I learn
the more I lean
away from celebration
and fall into mourning.

Do I love this land? Yes.
Do I celebrate its beauty? Always.
Do I need a break from labour
to break bread, snags and beers
with friends and strangers?
I have weekends for that.

If we can hold a candle
and sombre note
for fallen soldiers
on ANZAC Day,
can we not
smear bloody dirt on our faces and
bury our bare feet on broken soil
for as long as it takes
for the land to bear witness
to our spirits
that Terra Nullius is a lie
and my colonialist ancestors
stole, and continue stealing
from First Nation Peoples?

Can we not break
the radical back
of white supremacist hunger
that takes and takes and takes,
giving this day away
and reconciling our collective hearts
to those who lost their land and lives?

Cadell - My Youngest

With bodies on the studio floor
in Savasana.
Think of something pleasant,
she suggested.

As my eyes turned inward,
you were the first my heart found.
You, my son
with your gentle face,
mysterious eyes,
hair laying light
in the light that seems
to cradle you always.

You're the most beautiful creation,
my son. It is no surprise as a child
you spoke of seeing angels -
naming them and sharing giggles.
I have no doubt your name
still crosses their lips
with fondness too.

Minor Wisdom

Whole

Yes, you dropped
And hit the earth.
And yes, you cracked a little.
But you didn't shatter
Or break beyond repair.
Don't you see?
You didn't really fall apart,
You're still whole.

Practice Falling

Practice falling,
Beloved
Because you will
Fall
Like a tree
Like a star
Like a tumbling child
Like all things ambitious
Back to the earth
You will fall
Many times.
So, practice falling
Beloved,
So you can fall
again.

Too Much

Some days
   I drown.

I make life unbearable
with
  commitments.

Too many
  appointments.

Not on my calendar
  but on my conduct.

Expecting too much
 of myself.

Including:
  poignant,
  powerful
poetry.

Stand Still

But there was no fork in the road
No divergence in the woods
Instead, the road fell away
Into a wilderness
Into a desert
Into a grave
Into an undiscovered future
And a past I was running from
   So, I stood still
And waited
For the fierce storm in my soul
   To make way
For the bright and morning star

Body Angst

it moves to find your fingers and toes
travels across the marrow and bone
like a gavel, strikes your nerves with blows
and squeezes your lungs of all they hold.

Angst, you are welcome to visit, because you
have something to tell me...
but you cannot stay.

How to Carry the Sun

It's not every day you sail
into the sunset. In fact, it may be
that you've never sailed - in which case
you could find a place at dusk
facing the horizon
and just as the sun's gentle fingers
brush against the evening's curve
you could close your eyes
and be where you are -
a grateful witness
who, with tired sailors,
collect the day's waning warmth
like seashells
in a carefully cupped hand
for some time later.

Embodied

Body. Beautiful

be in your body
bold. beautiful.
branded by life and all that's moved
through its blood. bones.
babies maybe.
beauty blessed by you
and those who hold you
with the same envious
love and respect you
have for yourself.

take to task and cast out
dreamers and deadbeats
who dare separate
you from your temple
- as if it doesn't hold
the most sacred of souls.

screw the body-shamers
who, for colour, curve,
and calendar years
spin lies to assuage
their own failed attempts
of one day
holding their own head high
like you do
with all the style and strength
of one who
marched through hell
to recover the truth
that we are all
God's masterpiece.

Call Me a Girl

If crying in the presence
of loss or beauty
breaks the mould
you squeeze yourself,
and all men into,
call me a girl.

If expressing my inner world
through movement, music,
art and poetry
makes you squirm
'coz that stuff's dumb,'
call me a girl.

If defending the weak
instead of dominating them
like your insecurity demands
makes me weak too,
call me a girl.

If simply being me
doesn't fit into
the preconceived box
of what a man
should be
in all his independence,
toughness, sexiness,
straightness, attractiveness,
aggressiveness,

and all this disqualifies me
and all you can say
because all you heard
was 'don't be a girl' –
go ahead,

call me a girl.

I'll take it as a compliment.
I'll take it
you haven't taken the time
to really think it through –

How women birthed the world.

How women bled for you,
fed, held, taught and raised you.

How they never called a monopoly
on tenderness, emotions and beauty.

And how you've been boxed in
and can't see past
the blinding mask
you put on as a boy
to soak up the fear,
tears and deepest desire
to safely be
your very own self.

Sisters, Oh, Sisters

Sisters, oh, sisters
I applaud and revere
The way you hold
Strong hands
To the abandoned air
With courage and fire
Reclaiming
What has been yours all along -
Your embodied place
In this world.

Sisters, oh, sisters
I'm in awe of the way
You're coming home
To yourself
Writing poems of redemption
Stories of climbing back
From mountaintops
Scared stupid men,
And the spirit of the age,
Threw you from.

Sisters, oh, sisters
I am blessed by the places
You're calling home:
Your body
Your art
Your brilliance
Your sexuality
Your unexploited self
The divine gift that you are.

Sisters, oh, sisters
Rest assured
That amidst the men,
Marketers and ministers
Who think little of you,
There are husbands
Fathers, elders and sons
Who want nothing more
Than to see you roar
And lead the way
To a merciful
Future.

Wisdom for Living

Where to Build Your Home

I built my home
  in the hearts of others.
Trading my treasure
  for a seat at their table.
Placing my best self
  on the shelves of their acceptance.

This was a mistake.

They walked away.
I was no longer welcome.
I found myself homeless,
empty
wondering if
I had anything more to give.

Take heart,
 God whispered.
You have plenty more to give.
The emptiness came
to let you know
you simply built your home
in the heart of others
instead of your own -
with me.

Wounded Healer

Time doesn't heal in the dark.
Not in stale air
pregnant with shame.
Not over time like this.
Not ever.

It must be struck with light.
Given time in open air.
To sting again briefly.
To remind you, you're alive.
And this matters.
It always has.

Now, pain will return
for you to do the work,
together with love,
over time.

And you will mend
in the form of a wiser you.
One bearing nail-scarred hands.
A wounded healer.

Moving Home

If your bones and bruising need,
pause along the path
or pace a little slower,

In fact, ask the question,
who called me to walk this way?
You might find

you are the answer
but things have changed
and the best way forward

is to return.
And now the only person
you'll need

to negotiate with
is an earlier version
of your now wiser self.

Sorry

And then there are the things you long for:
the full womb
the mortgage approval
the ring with bent knee
the benign oncology results.

F#*k! you may say;
Oh God! you may pray;
...why others, and not me?

And of the things you take for granted,
all of the above
plus breathing
food choices
living relatives
running water
the cry of your child
the ability to read this
and a thousand other things

...you say nothing.

Thanks, at best.
But never sorry.
Sorry, I have what you long for.

Trauma, Know This

Trauma,
I refuse to believe
You came from nowhere,
Landing like a tattered angel
Marked for our destruction,
Seeding hell on earth.

You have a way
Of multiplying, masking
And holding a mirror
To every fault and failing -
Driving destruction
At full speed
Through generations,
Damn you!

The way you maim
And tame and carve
Your claws into
The timber of our existence,
Leaving brokenness
In your wake
Makes me pray,
'Oh God.'

I cannot fathom
A world without you
But I long for it
I long for it
I long for it
With every spinning cell
Of my sacred self.

Trauma, know this -
I will write, recover
And write again
With poets and healers;
Doing my part
To absolve you
Of your dark place
In every beloved soul.
So help me, God.

Break the Day

Break open the day
like it's a gift you hid from yourself
and forgot where it was
until one day,
this day,
you found it,
hidden in plain sight -
like God was playing
a sneaky trick on you.

Listen, there is plenty
to frown at
flip the bird at
and
tell to eff off
but
there has to be something
that comes to you
as a gift
today.

Your job is to find it.
Then,
tear that sucker open
like it's been missing
and there are a million smiles inside.

Throw the wrapping on the floor,
knowing your mum will collect it
after she asked you to do it five times.

Scan the room for siblings
with jealous looks
and give them the stink-eye.

This one is yours, baby!
You didn't earn it.
But you found it.
And it found you.
This day has come to you.
Break it open!

Light

Light strikes a man where he lays
not partial to his breathing
nor pigment
nor the way he strings a sentence
to describe its warmth.

Every day
light shines its fair rays
warming the smallest sapling,
budding forth
in the shelter
of its decaying ancestors
who made way for the light
with their falling.

.

SECTION 2

The Poetry Chapel Collective
Chosen Works

Deborah Blythe

When I was a kid contending with family, race, and religion, poetry found me. Poetry gave me a voice as an adult when I faced failure, when others failed me, when I felt displaced yet again. Poetry taught me that this human experience is exquisite and fallible, and ultimately worth noticing.

This is why I write poetry. I write to notice the ordinary, the extraordinary, the contradictions. I write to fight back and matter. I write to make peace with my experience and let others affect me. I write to believe in Goodness and in something beyond me.

I hope you find my poems isomorphic to life: tender, then unexpected, gut-wrenching, sacred, full of sound and fury, beauty and wonder.

Most days, you will find me sharing a casual charcuterie board with friends or my kid at sunset, wholeheartedly immersing myself in my latest and greatest endeavour, or sitting across from humans and holding space for our singular experiences as a therapist.

Find me on Instagram: @deborahblythepoet

Small

there will be days
too soon
where you will
stretch yourself into
the vast shadows of
adulthood

but for now
let yourself
be small
enough
to be held on a lap
by someone bigger
than you

Fail

One day you will fail
at what mattered most to you.

You never did a thing slow;
you were scared of being wrong
or even worse,
doing wrong
to someone along the way.

You wondered
if you were good enough
or smart enough
to be more than enough
(maybe even the best).

One day you will fail
at what mattered most to you.

You will find
you can't be enough
for the world.

So, you start over,

figuring out
what is
enough
for
you.

Walk

I cannot possibly
run
to the cemetery
today.

I could never
make it,
what with the
shovelfuls
of failed what-ifs,
and still to-dos
burying me,
a weighty reminder
with every tender,
wearied step,

and flashbacks to
that particular dark,
circling above my
head like a vulture,
closing in
waiting to
pounce at
any sign of
weak,

and a trigger-happy society
stretched out
before the path
like a minefield
volatile
to every matter
of heart and country.

So instead,
today,
I walked.

Heresy

is dignity in holding your gaze,
in the discomfort
and unspeakable spaces
between us

is holding the colors of love
with you who were told
yours isn't love

is struggling at home
alone
knowing your marriage
won't make it
this time

is quietly questioning
in the pew
too scared to leave
the current.

If it is
heresy,
let me be
for I am in
good company.

If God Were Here

If God were here,
I dare say
God would blow right past this
potentially irreverent and offensive
suppositional phrase I just uttered
and sit with me
on this piano bench
long enough

(perhaps too long),

until I knew.

Lisa Dodge Pinkham

Participating in this collective has been a profoundly stretching and prolific experience. I hold David and all the courageous participants in highest regard.

Vocationally, I have been involved in dance & health education, college ministry, spiritual formation, cardiac rehabilitation, health and life coaching, home-schooling and best of all, being a mom to two amazing daughters.

I am passionate about fostering intimate and authentic relationships with God and others. Currently, I facilitate online communities of practice who integrate storytelling, neuroscience and prayer in relationally safe spaces where joy and sustainable transformation is normative.

My book, Real Talk with God: How to Get Your Head Out of the Ditch of Despair, is available in printed form and audiobook. Find me on my Youtube channel, LisaDodgePinkham.

I graduated from Gordon-Conwell Seminary with an M.A. in Religion and University of New Hampshire with a B.S. in Exercise Physiology with Dance and Psychology minors. A native New Englander, I raised my family in Virginia for seventeen years and now reside in Maryland with my husband of thirty years.

Please Stay

Oh no, dear kindness, please don't go.
We didn't mean to kick you out of the human race.
It was just a gradual forgetting and letting
other things crowd you out.

We assumed we could always find you
  at the back of the line
when we had more time.
We thought the few true heroes would keep you
  on the front page,
until we could make space for you
  in the back alley of anonymity.

We just didn't see that eyes still smile
even when mouths are hidden.
We just didn't learn to quiet our fear
so we could still hear your brilliant ideas
of how to share you in the
sacrificial simplicity of being our best selves.

We just weren't sure that you could guarantee
  a return if we spent our supply of you on others.
Self-protection eclipsed generosity.
And you fled even faster.

We refused to believe that you were self-propagating,
more prolific than rabbits and
more contagious than you-know-what.

Yes, it is true. You are not just a virtue.
We need you.
Please, kindness, give us another chance.

What If It Is Not All Your Fault?

That crushing weight you feel on your chest.
Shortening your neck.
Stealing your breath.
It's the judgment:
"This is all your fault."

But what if it's not?
What if you try on the idea that
perhaps it's not all your fault?

Like donning a hat and
parading around the store
before making the purchase,
or stepping through a revolving door
into an expansive spring meadow
surrounded by mountains,
or throwing your arms wide and
singing your silliest song
just for a few seconds.

You don't have to decide whether it's true or not.
Just notice what it feels like to
live as if it's not all your fault.

Shame

Awww, come on out, shame.
It is time we got to know you
and let you serve your purpose––
no more, no less.
We've called you by the wrong name.
Ignored you.
Tossed you at someone else like a hot potato.
We've exiled you,
even as we've locked you within.

Others have thrown the part of you that belongs to
them at us.
Blindsided, we've absorbed you
without sending you back to your original owner.

And what about the part of you that belongs to us?
Are you hiding under
that blue cloak of sadness,
red hoodie of anger or
camouflage of fear?

When you speak out of protection
and to promote change,
we drown you out with all that noise.

We overlook your contribution to our constitution––
our fearfully-and-wonderfully made-ness.
A little bit of you belongs in each of us.
Yes, even you.
Isn't it time we faced life together?

Reconcile

Dear	God
I don't want	this rift
between your	promises of
faithful kindness	and the stories
and gory images	of horrific
suffering	to become
irreconcilable	differences
between	us

You have already given me the
solution to this equation.
I will
snuggle up + share my anguish with you,
receive your comfort + listen to the stories you are
telling me.
I choose united hearts,
Yours + mine.
Instead of judgements,
theirs + mine,
I am okay with the unknowns in this
complex calculation.

Here and There

Dear one,
I know life feels hard enough here in this
confined space where you save your breath,
conserve your energy, wear your masks, and
tighten the valve to your heart.

But I am over here too.
Right here where judgements, persecutions, enemies and
curses abound.
Come on over and experience even more of me.
I will meet you with a storehouse of treasures.
You know ... every spiritual blessing ...
You will discover all the compassion, tenderness and
capacity for connection
that your heart contains.
You will gladly relieve the pressure of holding back
by opening that valve wide.
Swimming in the invigorating flow of
loving kindness
will make you come alive.
Dive in
and let me show you
what you and I are really made of.

But Now

When I heard, "My power is made perfect in weakness",
I thought it meant that *christ* was sitting on me,
squashing my deficiencies with his strength.
But now I see **You** sliding up close on a park bench,
wrapping **Your** arm around me and whispering
earnest confidence in my ear,
"You can do this. You and **Me** together. **We** got this!"

When I heard, "As the heavens are higher than the earth,
so are my ways higher than your ways and my thoughts than
your thoughts",
I thought it meant that *god* stood towering above me,
shaking his scolding finger with the other
hand on his hip.
But now I see one arm open wide and the other
reaching down to lift me up.
I hear the words from **Your** generous grin,
"Come on up. Please, share this view with **Me**."

When I heard, "For you died, and your life is now hidden with
Christ in God",
I thought it meant that I lay crumpled in a tiny ball
with *christ* shielding me from *god's* disdain,
But now I see that **You** are the **Ones**
Rolling out the red carpet,
Distinguishing and delighting in my every detail,
As **You** sing, "Here Comes the Bride!"

Childlike wonder returns.
Expectant eyes open.
What will I see next?

2 Cor 12:9. Isaiah 55:9 Colossians 3:3

Amanda Dzimianski

I like to call myself a human learning how to be—how to be present, to be whole, to be loving, to be myself, and to be in relationships. I think this is the best work I will ever do. (Also the longest.)

I live in Northeastern Georgia, United States, near the city of Athens. Our home stands in the lands of the Yuchi, Muskogee/Creek, and Cherokee (Eastern Band) peoples. I am a certified writing coach, full-time parent to two brilliant and beautiful little boys, homeschool teacher, partner to my closest friend David, and a firm believer in the power of the small space.

I'm a lifelong writer, but had no idea I was also a poet until the summer of 2021. Looking back, I see so many places where poetry was stirring under the ground and sneaking up above the surface through cracks created by wear, tear, and time. The pandemic was an earthquake that widened those fissures in me enough to let the light in.

The opportunity to write with the Poetry Chapel collective came at just the right time, and I am so grateful to have met each of the other authors. It's been an honor to bear witness to the stories and words they've shared.

My poems explore religious deconstruction, personal autonomy, and creation as participation in Divine goodness.

You can connect with me online at
amandadzimianski.com,
and on Instagram @amanda.idareyoutospellit.

Empty

what is it like to be empty?

to have no words left to give
or gifts left to offer
or hope left to live?

it's like
embracing shadows
believing
whispered stories
about what's real
learning the ending
leaves you hollow-chested

or like
capturing sunlight
with both palms
feeling warmth
then finding them unfilled

emptiness
is feeling
the ache
of bare space,
tracing the room's
edges
and catching the
e c h o e s
remembering
what used to
hold place

but this we know:

abundance
means
we've known
the taste
of scarcity

silence
teaches us
to listen for
a better song

and becoming
empty
is the first step
to being filled

Treasures

stained face,
clasped gently
in my damaged palms,

listen:

wholeness
hasn't meant
never unmade

do you know
broken glass
builds
precious pearls?

you are
grace -breathed and -born/e

you
paint joy
across cosmic core

and I am
gold
shining through
your every
costly
crack

What We Forget When We Talk About Spring

we're fixated
on the bursting forth
and less on the force
of the birth

we forget the washouts
erased paths
and root-ripping rainstorms

we forget the mud
sucking at our soles
clinging to clothing

we forget the struggle
below the surface
the life writhing up through soil
scuffling skyward
just to catch a frigid breath
bathe in the light
before a quick death
by freeze

remember, my soul—
escaping the clutch of winter
exacts a cost
and spring is made of more than thriving

who says springtime is not exactly where you are?

Watermarks

it's that kind of day
the kind where you pull out the books
and leaf through the pages
the water-stained pulp slicing a cut or two
across a not-tough-enough
fingertip
while the rain spits and slides
down the windowpane

the kind where the silent memories
scream inside your mind
and you watch the tapes (because you're that old)
then rewind and repeat
and this remembering rubs your soul raw,
this watching all the wrong—
theirs and yours

yeah, it's that kind of day
and all the wealth and all the joy and all the light
got sucked right into your ledgers
             with their neat columns and precise rows,
                    the spreadsheet-like cells
                           forming a very elegant
                                        prison

        there's a knock on the door of your dusty room
                        and there stands a Friend,
                          the one who doesn't speak
                          but their eyes sing kindness

they walk to the heavy-laden
table, look down at thin sheets
thick with grievance and grief
misdeed, misstep, misunderstanding.
they pull from their deep pockets
a bottle of blood-red ink
and suddenly
all those careful columns are awash & unmoored
letters floating free in a sea of
wet, unflinching witness

you watch the flood drown your pages
then drip by drop, crimson color disappears
and on those record sheets
the sins are rewritten
unhealed pain put on display
a grasping for enough
bathed in generous compassion
and the old language scratched out
by an ancient mercy

all of it
gilded by grace
smoothing out
the watermarks of shame

today, your Friend called and left a card, and signed it,
Love

Vivien Firth

Born in the fifties in industrial North East England I was impacted by the love of Jesus when I was fourteen. I believed that if someone loved me enough to die for me then all I wanted was to live for Him.

I had to leave school six months later to help look after the home and my three younger brothers when my mum left. Through attending a local technical college one day a week, I was able to gain secretarial qualifications which opened the door for my first employment as a bank manager's secretary. At twenty-five, I left work and home to go to Bible College. From there I was sent on mission to various counties of the UK, one of which was Yorkshire––where I now reside with my wonderful husband. After college, I worked as a secretary to the Archbishop of York and his chaplains and, after completing an Honours Degree, I served for twenty years as a Methodist minister. God miraculously provided for mission trips to Romania, Kenya, Israel, the Caribbean Islands, Wales and South Korea.

Being part of this Poetry Chapel has been a great privilege and adventure. David Tensen's amazing mentoring has enabled me to make miracle reconnections with family and friends through the creative language of the heart.

My prayer is that you encounter something of the transformational love of God in my poems which I believe is available for all who dare to journey on faith's wild adventure.

How Much He Loves You

It's not what you profess
or how you dress
that makes God love you.
It's not what you do
nor answering,
"who are you?"
that makes God love you.

You are loved by Him
without condition or contrition,
because He is the One
who rescued you
before you knew
He could love you.

You are His prize
and in His eyes, beyond the wise
His love grew you.
For He has always loved you.

He is reaching
for your heart.
So He can restart
where you left off
and show you
HOW MUCH
He loves you.

At Mercy's Door

In a world of Make-Believe
And masks
Manipulation becomes the
Task Master
That drives
And lies
Until you have forgotten
Who you really are!

Tethered to lies and tasks
That mask
Deception's deadly depths
Give no Rest, no drive
Only Lies
Distress, Discontent
Self rejection and confusion:
Who am I, really?

Breaking point at last is reached
Lies smashed
Truth confessed
Truth that wounds
Before it heals,
Making reconciliation possible:
Finding who I really am
At Mercy's Door.

The Joy of Letting Go

Let Your thoughts like waves
wash over my soul,
breaking addiction's
desire to control,
to live in the past
a victim of genes and scenes
of sadness and slavery's dream,
time's tormenting wheel
of rotating emotions
so unrelenting and real.

Like rocks in sand
let me roll back
with the tide
Anger locked into the seaweed of time
Inadequacy as driftwood
that floats back
to the sea
I let go of all that troubles me.

As the waves wash back in
to the sandy shore,
I lift my soul once more
in humble adoration
of the miracle
of Transformation——
the joy of letting go
to imagine a new horizon.

Let Me Breathe the Essence of Heaven

When all else fades
And all I see
Is the wonder of You
And none of me

When in the silence
I breathe pure air
And nothing else matters
But knowing you're there

My heart skips a beat
To know you are near
All anxiety gone
And nothing to fear

The mystery of heaven
Can now be known
As we kneel to worship
Before Your throne

Breathing the essence
Of heaven is this:
Lost in Your goodness
Filled with Your peace

Overcomers

Not just painted over for a year
But sponged out forever
All my guilt
and stains
For my Saviour became
the Scapegoat
forever
and
for all.

He was presented alive
and sent into the wilderness
there to defy
the tempter's lies
By the power of the Word
like a majestic bird
soaring on thermal heights
He shows us how
to rise as
Overcomers.

*"And they overcame by the blood of the Lamb,
and by the word of their testimony:
and they loved not their lives unto death."*

(Revelation 12v11)

A Child of Joy

Do winters have to be so long?
Does it take a worldwide crisis to
Awaken springtime in our soul?
Or does the effervescent joy of youth
Spin round from its beginning to the end
To make the wintertime a friend?

How is it that it takes so long
To recognise the tune, the song,
The laughter, and the rain
In childhood's intermittent pain?

Does every season hold perhaps
A building block of preparation
For God's miracle of reclamation?

To find as life's wheel has turned,
We have come full circle
To discover who we really are:
A Child of Joy.
For even when you're old and grey
Your Heavenly Father will say,
"My Child, I love you.
In the winter and the spring
And all the seasons in between.
You are mine and will forever be
Throughout all
Eternity."

Suzy George

I can barely remember a time in my life without a book in my hand. Words and sentences were like the oxygen to my soul while I endured many traumatic experiences as a child. Words and sentences transported me to other places, fed my insatiable curiosity and taught me about a world I was often isolated from due to extreme religious beliefs.

I spiralled into trauma-induced darkness in my early thirties and as I slowly began feeling my way out, I reached for that soul oxygen. As I began breathing again, words started to form into poems to help make sense of the experiences I was having.

These pages holding my poems are hugged on each side by beautiful souls who I've been privileged to journey with as part of Poetry Chapel. During this rich, rewarding journey, I have watched the authors' hearts pour onto the paper which you now hold in your hand.

I live in Adelaide, Australia with my two beautiful children, a dog called Maverick and a cat called Cici.

I have written around 150 poems but this is my first published collection.

If you enjoy these poems, you can find more of my work on Instagram @ light_and_day_poems.

Word by Word

I will not write
for finger clicks, claps
or loves and likes
pressed on me
through a screen.

I will not write
just buzzwords,
for followers or fame.

I will not perform
for consumptive crowds
demanding:
Entertainment.
Titillation.
A popularity contest –
"May the most woke win."

I will write for this:

A tender heart space.

Giving voice
to the muted.

Speaking of
ordinary magic
in every day.

Letting pain
leak out.

Word
by
word
it will
become
something.

A Walk with Five-Year-Old Me

There's no going back
but I'm taking you with me
to this tree I pass on my walk
where often I've wanted
to hang a rope, but today
I'm going to use that rope
to make a special swing
for you.

I'm flying through the air.
Stomach dropping to my toes.
I'm singing:
'I don't care if there's a fire,
I'm just going higher,
till I reach the big blue sky'.

Together we're flying.
There's no going back;
Now we travel together.

Sacred Inhabitation with Five-Year-Old Me

There's no going back
but I'm taking you with me
to this holy place where
once you were lost and
blinded by cult culture:
shame, fear and fire
as the only currency.

We've been through
trial, trouble and trauma.
But now that I've found you,
my dear,
we're going to
dance barefoot

In wide-eyed wonder,
letting grace and love
freely declare

This body,
this space
we share together

This
right here
is
holy
ground.

A Blessing for the One Who Grieves

A blessing from
one grieving heart
to another.

Blessed are/is your:

Eyes. Releasing rivers of tears;
watering the soil of your heart
to seed new meaning.

Hands. Held open enough
to let go and
bless what was.

Mouths. Bearing witness to
all the good, graceful and
sacred pain of grief.

Rage. Freely expressing
what it needs to say,
to speak of the injustice.

Acceptance. What was and is;
holding space for all
the unexpressed love.

For the One who mourns today,
You are called Blessed.

Failure – contemplation version

See how
clouds scud,
the world spins, and
birds sing.

You failed.
That terrible thing
happened.

Yet, you
are still here, and
this breath
is still moving
in
and
out.

This breath
is still moving.

This breath is.

This breath.

Breathe.

Kate Hughes

I only discovered poetry writing a few years ago. I'd taken myself on a retreat with Tozer's book, The Pursuit of God. (If you haven't read it yet, I highly recommend it.) Each day I read a chapter then would go and sit and stare at the ocean, contemplating what I had read. In these times of contemplation, I found myself praying in rhymes and writing simple poems.

Since then, I've found that poetry is a great way for me to connect with the Trinity. I really hear their voices when I meditate and write. Most of what I write isn't for public consumption, it's more my personal processing and conversations with the Holy Spirit.

Over the last few years, I have journeyed my father being diagnosed with cancer, his courageous fight and then him going to be with Jesus. Some of the poems I share on the following pages come with a trigger warning if you are grieving.

Being part of this poetry collective has been a beautiful experience. As well as learning more about the technical side of writing, it has forced me to make time and space to process.

I'm based in Bristol, UK, but as a west country girl, I spend as much time outside of the city as possible. When I'm not working or writing, you'll generally find me outside, halfway up a mountain or swimming in a lake.

Little One

Little one,
Knowing what
I know now
I wish I could protect you

Little one,
So many people
Will teach you
So many things about God that are untrue

It will often be inferred
That blessing
Is linked to your behaviour

You'll be told that
Any little slip up
Might make you
Slip out of grace

But this fragile view of grace
Is an insult to the cross

Little one,
You'll be told
That God expects
Perfection
Purity
Piety

Little one,
We made the mistake
Of thinking
That Christians own
Christ-like behaviour

When in fact
Perfection is unobtainable
Purity is a gift given
Over and over again

And (also)
Piety can go to hell
For we do not need to fear hell

So do not constrain yourself
Only looking for God
In church
Or
Amongst Christians

Know that He
She
Them
They
Can be found
Anywhere
And
Everywhere
That love is

Permeating all of creation

Unhealthy Processing

Cancer is a good reason to stop
Cancer is a good reason to start
Again
Picking up a smoky pacifier

When fear and worry overwhelm
I numb

A drink
A cigarette
A cigarette
A drink

Choosing my own annihilations
With every inhalation

Bowel cancer
Metastasized to liver
Stage four

Why him?
Why us?
Why ask?

There is no answer

Two years of quitting disappear
With a calming drag
I breathe in shame
Which mixes well with this pain

So I numb it
Bottle it
Hide it
Act strong

And if I can
When I can
I'll pray

(After Christian Wimen)

Bitter Sweet Dance

We prayed, like your life
Depended on it
Because it did

We prayed, hoping your life would
Continue
But it didn't

We constantly feel
The loss of you
Because the gift of you
Was so big

This pain,
This pain is now
A part of me
And it is oddly
Bitter sweet

Bitter
Because life stolen early
Is a travesty
Yet
Sweet
Because it represents
All we shared
Every laugh
Every tear
Every dance
Every comfortable silence

So now
Some days
I can smile in gratitude
That we ever got to be
Yet
Other days
It hits me, a tsunami
An ocean of grief

But
When grief's black hole beckons
I cling to land
With a picture of you
Partying in heaven
Not quite so dead
Instead
Eternally alive

Kate Kim

My birthplace is a beautiful seaport village in Inchon, South Korea. My family immigrated to Minnesota when I was 7 so my fondest childhood memories are of diving at the lake and sledding on snow days. We made a big move again when I was 15 and my home has been sunny Southern CA since. All the moving around made my heart good soil for the Gospel--thirsty for belonging, identity, and meaningful purpose. I ended up marrying a pastor and I have loved serving in the church in various ways. And now as our four boys are leaving the nest, I have been leaning into God's call to be a Spiritual Director. This vision for the next season of my life gives me great joy!

I have always had a deep love for words and kept a journal since childhood. In them, my prose often weaved in and out of poetry, especially when life felt overwhelming. So, after years of caretaking, and abruptly losing my father and then my mother 2 years later, I sought consolation from the Psalms and other poets to process a myriad of emotions. By God's grace and providence, I found David Tensen and this compassionate community of poets.

Poetry has been my pathway to healing and a deeper connection to my own heart and other grieving, longing, and tender hearts. I hope to continue writing and help others feel less alone too.

You can find me on Instagram @blessedwithsons.

New Wine

Finally, I stopped at a park
on a sunny spring day,
after that long, long mind-numbing winter of grief.
After that frenzied fall of regret.
After those two summers of death.
First, dad leaving too soon.
Then, mom's long goodbye.
Each rearranging the seasons
and changing the horizon of my life.

And for the first time
in a long, long time,
I felt unbound by time.
I lingered a bit longer,
even found a bench and sat down.
Up, across, far, and wide
I was surrounded by so much green.

Suddenly my gaze shrunk back
when I felt a familiar tug.
I saw that my heavy heart had caught up to me.
I asked her if we could stay awhile.
I lifted her up and plopped her down next to me.
Her weight brought tears to my eyes and we just sat,
enjoying the trees with leaves dancing in the wind,
amused by the birds prancing about on the grass,
admiring the rosebuds smiling shyly at us.

Then I felt the warm breeze
move the hair out of my eyes,
dry my tears and cradle my heart.
I heard my little heart let out a long, long sigh.

And into the silence,
we both whispered to God,
I feel homesick. I miss her cooking. I miss his smile.

Then I asked the tree with leaves dancing in the
wind
What time is it?
He replied, *It's time to dance.*

I asked the birds prancing in the grass
What time is it?
They replied, *It's time to sing.*

I asked the rosebud smiling shyly at me
What time is it?
She replied, *It's time to bloom.*

Then we asked Jesus, my heart and I,
What time is it?
He smiled and with a twinkle in his eye,
He replied, *It's time to be drunk!*

It's time to raise a glass to spring!
You've reached the dead end of despair
and found hope's garden,
where regret is the best fertilizer.
Stop measuring and recounting.
Why pay penance for what has been paid?
Bury duty.

Rest, delight, plant new seeds.
Live abundantly.
You don't have to hide.
Abide, abide, abide.

It is time
      to be drunk
            on new wine.

Nostalgia (for Dad)

Nostalgia eclipses my heart
and I realize I have been
living with longing all my life.

Watching Gilmore Girls reruns,
teenagers going to a Bangles concert,
I am transported to a time
when I longed to be carefree,
instead of delivering pizza
with Dad in a maroon Pontiac
so we wouldn't go bankrupt.

Flashbacks of us riding up
in our yellow station wagon
with a wooden trim
to a Dairy Queen on a
humid Minnesota summer day.
Little brother in his short shorts
and me in a polyester sundress
Two Blizzards and a Peanut Buster Parfait
every time.

But today what I wouldn't give
to sit with you in a car and go through
a carwash,
a drive-thru,
a drive-in,
or even to a doctor's appointment.

Somewhere between
old habits and new beginnings,
between nostalgia and longing
is where I'll find you
still here with me.

A Strong Tower (for Mom)

Mom held our family together
and I was her helper.
We were especially good at playing
the family Jenga game,
carefully building a life
around the hurt,
placing
    one
  layer
   after
another
     hoping
  nothing
    would
   fall.

Now I am the only one left,
and it seems all has fallen
but when I look back,
I see God was playing
with us too,
filling all those gaps,
grace upon grace,
with His love.

I see now
all those memories
have become
a strong tower
that I can always run to,
until we all
meet again.

Every Step

It's true
what they say
about grief.

It seems like hearsay
and you don't really know
until you know.

Grief is an ocean.

You think you can dip your toes in
and feel it just a little.
Maybe even let it swell above your ankles;
surely it will stay below your knees.

Then an unexpected wave
knocks you over
and you are drenched
head to toe.

Still, it's better to take your chances;
you can't miss out on the ocean.
It will never give up on you
and every step
is an arrival.

Resurrection Hope

Newly unfurled neon leaves
lining the streets
feel like baby skin
on my fingertips.
Sunbursts of color
on flowering bushes and succulents,
even the prickliest cacti.
Weren't they a shriveled brown
just yesterday?

They remind me of resurrection hope.

But so does the cane,
the walker and wheelchair
stored in my garage
I've decided.
They may evoke memories
not so pretty
but they got us through
the harshest winter.

And now they will point to
the most glorious of worlds
like the one
on the other side
of that magical wardrobe,
where bodies once broken
are running free among the daffodils.

Keally Kweyama

Ever since I can remember, Jesus, family, and all things creative have not only saved my life but given it all its meaning. Growing up in Melbourne, Australia, I was fortunate to be surrounded by people that grew and celebrated my love for these things.

I have found immense healing through creative expressions, especially my writing.

Reading and writing poetry has quickly become a way I experience God deeply and my favorite way to describe Him. I find that sometimes, what can be difficult to say verbally, can better find its way out through paper and a pen.

I have been so impacted by being a part of The Poetry Collective. It is really such a joy to have learnt from David and to have grown alongside other incredible poets, let alone now be published in the same book as them! It has encouraged me to believe in my writing and to value what I have to say.

I hope that as you read my poems, you too will be encouraged and, perhaps, experience God the way that I did when writing them.

I now live in Northern California, USA, with my husband.

You can find me on Instagram: @keally.kweyama

Falling

Falling again,
Next to you

Not deep sleep
Kind of falling

The kind where
I find myself wondering,
Where am I?
And
Where was I going?

Falling in
Love
Dear husband.

For the first time
And then, again.
And fifty years later,
Then, again.

With the way you fall asleep,
Next to me
And wake up in the same place,
Next to me
Then, between sleepy snores,
Looking for me.

With our morning coffee
And kisses that feel like a spring breeze,
A taste I hope will never leave.

Is this what they meant by,
Joy comes in the morning?

You are the cap, crest and
Crown of the mountains

The sun that sets behind them,
And the ocean that mirrors them.

The roses in bloom
Like sweet perfume.

I look around to see
All that is lovely,
And captivating.

And
I am convinced,
Selfish it may be,
But
Maybe
It was created
Just so *I* would have words
To describe *you*.

Cave In

Slow down.
Trust,
That the world
Will not cave in -
If you are not
The one
To hold it up.

My God, My Home

Before I close my eyes
His are the last I see.

Forehead pressed against mine.
Drawing close.
Eyes transfixed.

And I am consumed.
Swallowed whole.
Beyond the point of no return.
For His love is abounding -
His eyes never withholding.

So, I close my eyes
For I am home.

Dear Ocean

Dear Ocean,
Tell me,
Do you ever refrain from raging and roaring?
Do you struggle to stay still in the silence?

You are a vast wonder,
Contrasting treasure and terror.
Containing beauty in every season,
Each one, no less beautiful.

Unpredictable Ocean,
Tell me,
How are you not afraid of mess?
How are you void of control?

I find comfort that
You were here long before me,
You will remain long after,
And I am immensely small.

And I am beginning to think perhaps,
There is an ocean within me.
Longing to be loud, to be seen
An ocean, still and serene,

Vast and full of wonder,
Treasure and terror,
Containing beauty in every season,
Each one, no less beautiful.

The ocean in me, embracing mess
Uncontrolled and uncontrollable
Unashamed of my need for the sand.
Yes,
I still need you to hold my hand.

My Dear Ocean.

Marianne Lienard

I grew up in a small Finnish town between lakes and forests. The world was beautiful at hand and beyond reach. There I came to faith in Christ between practicing judo and sewing clothes. After finishing my studies, I moved to Germany in the '90s and married. I have two children and am widowed. I'm engaged in volunteering through outreach street work in marginalized groups (cooperation with Neues Land e.V.) and in healing prayer (Heilungsräume Hannover e.V.).

I love to see seasons change, I love cats and different people. I like minimalism and things that are decoratively useless, I like learning new things and traditions which never change. I am an observer of life with bursts of social activity. Life is rippling blue waves and snowy deserts and both are so enjoyable.

Words opened fields and caves, ingredients and instructions, oceans and occasions for me as I learned to read. I wrote day and night: diary entries and nightmares, prose and poems in Finnish vowely words. My motivation to participate in Poetry Chapel was to find the unspoken words inside of me and try to get them out. The journey was amazing. I was midwifed in English language and lovingly welcomed in by David Tensen's exceptional, structured and caring mentoring and the amazing fellow writers.

My poetry is also found on Instagram
@marianne.liena

Winter Walk

The walkway chose us.
It is familiar.
So we walk

This warm, windy walk along the fields
with recurrent oncoming traffic
of oncoming illness.
I hear: Wie geht es?
A bit challenging, danke, ein wenig herausfordernd.
I whisper for mercy to come.

So we walk on, despite the oncoming traffic
of illness.
The tires compress the soil,
destroy the structure,
reduce the yield.
What can we hope for on this walkway?

Three magi women sat suddenly
        on the bench, disguised
        as Kurdish women with their
        gowns of red and blue velvet and gold,
        planning their presents for
        the coming King.

Marianne Lienard

Flesh Becomes Words

Before I close my eyes,
the daily tetris,
fun of the awkward kind begins.
Ich versuche mit den Dingen umzugehen,
and try to rearrange the wailing wall.

Carefully,
I move the lower cases of my sorrow,
patiently I put the bins of pain below.
Tenderly,
I thrust the trunks of trauma,
shove synonyms of past shadows around.

My beloved cryptographic boxes,
my tearfully sealed time machines.
My memories of the man of sorrow
Ja rakkaat raskaat surun kappaleet.

Before I close my eyes, then word by word
the bodies of the pain now excarnate.
Word by word
my scars write down their story
till every pain is taken

by the Savior
who
makes me
incarnate.

When you were 5

No evidence of
your appearance when you were five years old.
You are three and a half
in the summerly photographs
with your little brother,
then
nothing
until your first school pictures appear.

Afterwards, you would tell
about porcelain plates flying and
Apollo landing in the television room.
If it was funny, it couldn't be so bad
or so sad.
After all, you told many stories.
Your imagination was vivid.
You dreamed of wolves and bears fighting,
saw deep inside their throats and survived.

You moved.
Mummin ja ukin talossa,
the sun always shone in the living room.

Your bed was always wet in the morning.
But otherwise you were quiet and easy.
You didn't understand what happened.
You learned that there are many things
you don't understand.

Fedora

His shrink succeeded.
Followingly,
his black fedora
became too big.
First covering his face,
then shoulders
and ultimately his knees:
hindering
protecting
warming
so
cosy
so
lonely
so
black.

Tiny house fedora. Too tiny.

Your hair grew under the fedora.
Your thin hair grew.
Your hair with split ends,
your split thoughts.

Whose hat was it anyway?

Take off the hat, hinfort mit Dir!
Let the wind blow your mind
and your wild thin split-end bad day hair
for it is yours.

What Time Is It?

A tree dances
slowly in the March wind.
Dry. Wrinkled. Infertile.
Dead seeds hanging,
Empty promises of what can
no
longer
be.

Wait.

Come
closer
...
...
...
What looks like gnarls are buds, rivers of sap,
emerging life.
I am an old tree in March wind.
What can no longer be,
is.

Marianne Lienard

My Beautiful Garden

The brown twigs of my weeping willow
lie on the grass
like throwaway legs
Where should they even go?
the dead bones of last year's plans

Thank God he places winters
in the rhythm of time
and makes space for new dreams
new legs
new summers

Elizabeth Ma

I grew up in Hammond, Louisiana; a small, charming town with a little strip mall, where an exciting Friday night usually meant walking around Target. I attended LSU for graduate school and now work as a social worker––a field I take great pride in. Growing up, I had so much empathy for people that it overwhelmed me. I always seemed to be the person which others would talk to about their problems so, when it came to choosing a profession, social work just made sense.

Before I could afford therapy, I had poetry. In many ways, it saved my life. I started writing poetry after experiencing extreme health issues that left me traumatized. With no one to turn to, I turned towards writing. I used it as a means to process and grieve. It was like coming up for air. I kept writing poetry to process everything from God to my childhood. This is my first time sharing my writing in any form or fashion. I am excited and a bit nervous!

My hope is that some of the poems I am sharing connect with you and help you as much as they have helped me. If you would like to get in touch with me or would like for me to help give a voice to your experiences and write a poem for you, please email me at elizabethirenema@gmail.com.

Winters Never Last

When I was at the end of my rope
He saved me
Time and time again
When it seemed
I couldn't go on
I kept going on.
And He was there with me.

So pull on your history.
Every time
It seemed
Impossible
You made it.
And that rope
Ended up being longer
Than you thought it was.

One thing I do know is
Winter does not last forever.
Although it tricks you into believing it is eternal
It is only a season
   That will pass
   As suddenly
   As it came.

Science

Science tells me
I'm being punished for my childhood

That my immune system
Is attacking itself
Because of my trauma
That I lived tortured growing up
Wondering when the next fight
Would be the last fight
Constant state of flight or fight mode

And now
The sudden pain making me unable
To walk to the bathroom
Or take care of myself
Is because I was born
Into an unsafe home

Now science,
Can you tell me
How to heal?

God Needs No Convincing

You do
not have to
twist
God's arm
hoping for
one drop of mercy.

You do
not have to
plead
with Him
to help
you.

You can
breathe
easy.

If something
isn't working
anymore,
it means
something else
is
coming.

You do not have to twist God's arm hoping for one
drop of mercy.

A Regular Day

Because on a regular day
I'm struggling to find the words
For the man with his head in his hands
As he sobs because today is the date he lost his
  sister two years ago
I'm wondering how to motivate a nineteen-year-old
Scrolling through TikTok, resistant to vulnerability

I can reassure a stressed woman
Taking her seat worried she was five minutes late
It's not a problem

And I feel pleased when I
See those pink crocs with spikes
Propped up on a chair
Because I know light-hearted teasing
Will soon reverberate throughout the room

Tired of being depressed and
depressed because you're so tired
Good thing I know attempting to cheer someone up
only reflects your own discomfort
Sitting in pain

Taking a sip of coffee
Because the smell of lunch from the cafeteria is
making me hungry
And I'm listening to the clock ticking
looking forward to break because
I'm hoping the smell of fresh air
  will bring fresh energy
As we unpack the day's sorrows (again)

Present Over Regret

As I crave
  stability and roots,
   I am missing the
     beauty of the in-between

That is right in front of me.

I don't want to
  create more regrets
   by spending all
     my time

Thinking about all my regrets
  up until this point.

So
  relax
    and
      rest.

You won't regret it.

The Ups and Downs

This world has brought me many things.

It's brought me to my knees.
Not because I was praying
but because I couldn't breathe
  from the pain.
  from losing someone dear.
  from a diagnosis I couldn't bear.

This world has brought me many things.

It's brought me hope
that I would find another way.

It's brought me joy
when I was sharing a meal with friends.

It's brought me peace––
peace within myself and with others.

And it is also true
that this world
has brought me to pray.
To pray for enough strength
and grace for each day.

I can't wait to see what the world
  will bring me next.

Kate Rife

I currently reside in Northern California but ventured out here all the way from Omaha, Nebraska where I grew up and originally found my love for writing. Even as a young girl, I have always been one to wear my heart on my sleeve, and think and feel very deeply about the things we walk through in life and endure in relationships. I have never been able to articulate those thoughts and feelings quite like I have through writing and, in particular, poetry. It has allowed me to slow down and be present— with myself, with the people around me, and more importantly, with God. Essentially, I write to process these things and my hope for you reading is that you feel permission to as well. To hold what matters, let go of what doesn't, and find God in the midst of it all which you'll read about in the following pages.

For two years, I tried to abandon my writing altogether for fear that my voice would not make a difference. Luckily, when I was faithless, God remained faithful and placed people around me who continued to believe in me even when I could not believe in myself. I am forever grateful for the Poetry Chapel, as one of the first major steps into regaining some of that belief in myself again and getting excited about my future endeavours with writing.

To read more of my poetry, follow me
on Instagram: @katerife_

Five-Year-Old-Me

You sat
hopping from lap
to lap
hearing story
after story
Not watching
the time
but watching the one
holding you, holding onto
the words
that taught you
how to dream

Now I pray,
to be someone to hold you
to be a lap that
five—year—old me
would feel comfortable
to dream in
and
I pray,
to not watch time
but to watch the one
holding me, they're
the same hands
that held the loved ones even before
five—year—old me

When I'll Know I'm Loved

One day.
When a man comes along
and instead of hugging goodbye
he hangs on, I'll know
this
is not meant
to be
let go.

Patiently Waiting

Time passes me by
waving goodbye ... or is it a hello?
I can't seem to tell.
All I see is her
moving beautifully.

Swaying as she goes
lifting her arms high above
and down low—
Twirling
her steps close.
Holding her balance
and all my attention

Is she beckoning me to come closer?

Perhaps it is neither hello nor goodbye
All I know is
time is
an elegant dancer.
Perhaps that is
all I am to know
for now.
I should just join the dance

Perhaps this is
patiently waiting.

Holding You

Holding you
felt like
holding the world

So I let you go

Because I can't be
Your Savior, when
I need one too.

Goodbye Was Worth It [Excerpt]

If goodbyes were
as easy as
hellos, then
I would not dread
your footsteps becoming
leftover
   footprints
in my home

Perhaps then I wouldn't mind
seeing
   you go

But if
saying goodbye
   to you
is not easy, then
I know
our time together was
well spent.
Making me look forward
to seeing you again
and
saying goodbye to you
worth it all
   in the end.

Communion

i don't care
how you come

just as long as
you do.

to have you,
to hold you,

to know you,
i do.

Katy Roth

Words came to life when I began journaling as a pre-teen. A dimly lit ember continued to smolder when I filled in the final page of my first journal and closed it. I soon filled over thirty journals with scribblings, screaming words to myself and to God. Then one day, the words started to give life back to me. It came as a surprise.

The first poem I ever wrote was completely unexpected. I've learnt that God knows PRECISELY how to communicate with us. That first poem led me to read my words aloud to an audience of strangers at a church worship service. A breeze had picked up and began to blow across that ember. The first flame was realized; I devoted myself to writing daily—gathering twigs to keep that flame going.

I did not identify as a writer or a poet at that time. However, the words just kept coming as profusely as tears while I walked through a devastating season of losing my dad. I realized that God had given me a tool for my own healing. And He gave me a vision of writing in seasons of questions, doubt, and heaviness for others. A journey of honesty, freedom, and healing.

I am still healing and searching and reaching and learning. I will never forget the day that God gifted me with an invitation to feel my feelings. Consider these poems an invitation to do the same.

For more poems, writings and a link to my blog, follow me on Instagram @kbug8787

Alright Tonight

I wind my feelings on spools as thread
Tightly wrapped in cotton's stead
Considering my current plight
I suppose I'll be alright tonight

Shades of scarlet, green and blue
Passion, jealousy, sadness too
My gaze tilts up towards heaven's light
Perhaps I'll be alright tonight

Kneeling down, I pluck each dandelion,
Blow my cares towards the King of Zion
My eyes fixated I squeeze them tight
And for now, I'll be alright tonight

Beside the river I'll gather stones
And build an altar of my own
The smoothest pebbles will stack just right
And surely, they'll be alright tonight

I'll trace the skyline up above
Reminded of preeminent love
And though it tarries, this endless fight
I'll know that I'm alright tonight

Katy Roth

Sticks and Stones

Some problems are like pebbles or twigs
In your shoe
Those are the type
I brush off with a shrug
While hauling this boulder––
Shouldering it up my mountain
Of defeat

I can see your irritation
That sore spot from the dull
Pain pressing into your
Tender sole (soul)

Meanwhile, the sweat upon
My brow
Blinds me and
The scorching heat
Insults my incline

As I decline
To acknowledge the stick
On the path
Along our shared way

Tell me of your sticks and stones
And I'll roll this boulder your way.

Rusted Chain

I ventured out and up the hill
Forgetting to take in what's around me
Empty bench, metal can,
Worn wooden post and rusty chain

Spattered color of a familiar kind
Less audacious, these flowers
So very subtle––their presence barely noticed

I liken myself to these
A breed of quiet & gentle spirits
That respond to the soft breeze and winks of sun
That's me

But life isn't like springtime anymore
I know that you treasure the quiet whisper
And waltzes with the wind

But the wind has picked up and the sun blazes
Past fires have cast an invisible haze
I set my gaze to the rusted chain

Worn out, weathered
Tired yet tenacious
Immovable, irrevocable
The wind quiets for a moment
Then angrily charges my stubborn stagnation

But I will not be moved
I have been worn through every season
And I might possess every reason
To let go & be blown away
Later cast to the dump

But this chain has a place
And a grace all its own

Fragile

As you approach––
be careful

Why, you may ask?

I'm glass today
I'm not up for this task today
I wear a different kind of mask today

and

This face––
while you don't see a trace
of tears etched right in

I've been walking through mire
my composure expired
prepared to retire

I have nothing left to give
lacking energy to live
so, you'll have to forgive
my fragile composure

It's all a facade
my toughness has thawed
my nerves are all raw
and my functions are flawed

So again, I ask––
be careful as you approach

Webs

I bumped into kindness
In between pillars of defeat

In my rush to tend
To another fire
Kindness required

Nothing

I scoured my destitution
For some words
An offering

But kindness
Did not require my
Softening

Kindness exists
In the desperate, desolate places

In war-torn faces
Running their own races

I witness traces
Of kindness

Spinning webs
Intricate webs
Beautiful webs

In between
These pillars
Of defeat

Joyce Soe

My heritage is of Chinese descent; I was born in Singapore; grew up in New Zealand; and now live in Melbourne, Australia. To some extent, I have always found myself at a crossroads: I am placed in the overlap between eastern and western cultures. My mind loves the apparent certainty of reason and logic just as much as my spirit yearns to explore the unknowns beyond rational thinking. Poetry, for me, is a way to express the things too nuanced to put into a box of pure reason, while still staying within the bounds of what feels most safe and familiar to me: words.

Before joining this Poetry Chapel, I never considered myself a poet. Song writing has been my main form of creative writing for years. As this group has helped me grow in confidence in writing poetry, I have found a similar, yet unique, source of catharsis I experienced through song writing.

There is a divine relief that comes with releasing that which you didn't know was within you. This relief is enrichened when the words and experiences are shared by others. I pray that you might find parts of yourself in my words, often birthed out of chaotic and confusing wrestling.

I would love to connect with you!
Instagram: @thats.soe.joyce

Naked and Small

We wear armour to impress, deflect,
and cover up: an appearance of strength in hopes
that no one will see through to our nakedness.

We shoot missiles to justify, defend,
and conquer: attacks launched from the need to prove,
and to divert their gaze from seeing our smallness.

What if we lived in a world
where to be naked and small
was a strength?

Instead of putting on pretences
and starting self-defensive wars,
we would find ourselves unarmed,
vulnerable, but at the same time,
safe.

Safe for our authentic self to be heard.
Safe to listen,
truly listen,
to the neighbours we have hurt.

For when we put down
our weapons,
we no longer enter
conversations with a threat.

Our words and actions
in our naked and small state
just might bring a ceasefire
to the wars within and between.

today, I choose to take off
my armour,
false confidence,
and performance.
i put away my missiles:
ego and misplaced knowledge.

i return to nakedness.
embrace my smallness.
for I came into this world just like this.

naked and small
i will live.

The Re-Proposal

Like a lover
You beckon me.
Drawing me in
with sweet melodies,
tunes that only
You and I
can hear.

Like a father
You welcome me.
Wrapping me in
Your arms,
sheltering me from
their gaze
their thoughts.

And yet,
I have rejected You
again and again.
Again and again,
You pursued me.

Like a runaway bride
I left you at the altar
threw my ring away
as I eloped with my pride.

So, why are You still chasing me?
Why do You still long for me?

Oh, my child,
I hear Your tender voice.
Your days on this earth
have worn down your soul.

For they taught you to believe
that you are only desirable
so long as your actions
meet their standards.

There is no standard
but love.
Perfect, unadulterated love
that stands in the chasm
between your weaknesses
and My arm
stretched out to you.

I have prepared a future
more beautiful than you know,
filled with melodies
just for your ears to hear.
A sanctuary where you will no longer hide.

I am here
for you.

Will you take my hand?

Puzzle

Pieces

What if
I told you
that to

hold onto

peace in uncertainty,
you don't have to put

the p i e c e s

back together?

What if
it was enough
to simply hold
one piece
at a time
and wait?

For the picture will
come together.

Before the Autumn Leaves Fall

I've been seeing green leaves turn to red,
been reminded of beauty even in what's dead.
I've been grieving the things of this past season,
even before all the leaves have fallen.

I've been watching the fiery red spread,
across singed arms of branches overhead.
I've been reminded that fire makes gold pure,
fire allows clay to mature.

I've marvelled at the golden hues of dying leaves,
as if loss and growth came easy to me.
Yet, I've found myself mourning
my own shades of green,
not ready to let go of comfort found in familiarity.

The truth is, as I've been leaving things of old,
it hasn't always been easy to rejoice in the new.

Then, I learnt that to survive the coming winter,
trees must lose their leaves in autumn.
Trees must lose their leaves.
Trees must lose.
They must grieve.

I know that after winter comes the flowers.
So I choose to rejoice in dying colours,
even before all the leaves have fallen.

Catherine Sharpe-Lewis

It took thirty-five years to recognise that I am an artist and storyteller at heart. Just like the Old Testament prophet Jeremiah, I have stood before royalty and found myself at the bottom of the darkest wells. But no matter where I find myself, proclaiming the beauty and goodness of God burns in my bones, demanding that I speak and create. A drifter who has lived in twenty-five houses, nine towns and two countries, it took ten years of active searching to pin down the chaos of my life as Borderline Personality Disorder (BPD).

I write for the love of words, and for the joy of inviting others into the technicolour world that BPD's intensity affords me. While a crazy ride, I am unwilling to give up the gift of feeling deeply. I am a teacher, a mother of children who teach me to be brave, and a creative learning to stretch my wings.

Always remember, somewhere in the deepest darkness, our wings are forming.

If you would like to connect with me, you can find out more about me at
Catherinesharpe-lewis.com.

The Life Well Travelled

Two souls diverged in a fractious life
And I,
Confused by the path that had paved my way,
I stood and looked as far as I could,
Found myself in the past with a critical eye.
Eggshells strewn, word bombs exploded,
Weapons I hadn't recognised as loaded
Criss-crossed our paths with their paper cuts,
Lemon juice, vinegar, and other vices,
And I,
I discovered I had used these devices!

And both souls that morning equally lay,
Unmarred by events that might
Tar them black:
Is there hope for another day,
Even though there is no going back?
I shall be telling this with a sigh,
Somewhere in the days and years forthwith,
Two souls diverged in a fractious life
And I,
I forged a path to travel by,
And I pray that it might be kindly.

(After Robert Frost)

The Gatherers

We are gatherers
The ones who pick up the broken bones
From the sticks and stones
And words.
And old souls, fallen by the wayside
Of life.
Hollows that look like eyes once alive,
Shells of people, not whole, but lovely
In their brokenness.
We are the ones who bring home
Empty souls
And place them in a safer place
To keep for what? For how long?
It matters not.
What matters is the seeing, the gathering,
Lives filled with
Remnants of love and life,
The traces of hope, a lingering
Ghost of a laugh
That might come from the
Shell.

(After Nina Bagley)

Fear & Awe

The weight of the world
Cannot fit in a tear.
Nor a scream.
Nor a sigh.

Eternity drags on forever.
And I am ... afraid.

He tosses the world
In His hands

Yet He knows my name.
It is on His palm,
And I am ... relieved.

The Herald

When the days are getting bitter
The depression out of hand
And the words, they scald like liquid ice
That carves a reprimand
On a soul already broken
On the shattered plains of life
And your sodden soul, it wonders
  If it's had enough of strife...

Let the wonder of your soul
Soak up the life of shattered plains
Brought back into communion
By the sodden, soaking rains
Break the soil, carve a path glacial in scale
Hand the land's depressions
Seed to bite into the meal
Of the lengthening of days:
It just might be this winter's eve
Has ushered in spring's praise.

Acorns: A Poem in Three Parts

Act I: Acorn

The sweetest little creatures peek
from out upon the Oaken trees
their little hats and shiny cheeks
peer shyly from behind the leafs.

Act II: Oak Tree

Majestic tower rises up
into the heavens high above
and with a mighty whisper sighs
his kingly love song to the skies.

Act III: Observer

Into the holy creaking woods
the listener stopped with awe and stood
"I will be that big one day,"
She hears the little acorns say.

The End.

An Unexpected Discovery

I am looking back on all the

Beauty

And am

Shocked to find

There is SO MUCH

Beauty.

My world has been

FULL of love.

Though the path has been

Long and rough.

Yet I

Finally understand

That

Love (actually)

Is

Enough.

Do you want to be part of a future
Poetry Chapel Book,
writing alongside David Tensen
and other authors?

You could be in the next collective;
writings, sharing, healing and learning through
poetry and publishing.

Limited spots per intake.

Visit www.poetrychapel.com
for more information.

SCAN WITH SMARTPHONE FOR URL
AND RELATED RESOURCES

WINTERS NEVER LAST
available in eBook.

Also by David Tensen:

The Wrestle

Poems of divine disappointment and discovery.

2020

So I Wrote You A Poem

Poems of empathy on life, loss and faith.

2021

The Saving I Need

Poetry Chapel Volume 1.

2021

Support the author by purchasing via
www.davidtensen.com

e: david@davidtensen.com

ig: @david_tensen
fb: /davidtensenwriter
tw: @davidtensen

About the Author & Editor

Australian poet David Tensen brings form and
beauty to our deep spiritual yearnings. Drawing
from decades of experience in pastoral care,
leadership and spiritual development, his poems
have found their way into hearts of many.
Raw, accessible, and prophetic, David's writings
uncover pain and bring healing to it.

David, his wife Natalie, and three children live in
Queensland, Australia.

Lightning Source UK Ltd.
Milton Keynes UK
UKHW010935270522
403618UK00001B/89